When You Run Out Of Soap

Fun Activities
For Children 4-7

Mary Rose Pearson

CSS Publishing Company, Inc., Lima, Ohio

To Billie Wilson, director of the Florida Christian Writers Conference —
a gracious and wise lady, who has provided much help for
Christian writers, from beginners to professionals.

For more information about CSS Publishing Company resources, visit our website at www.csspub.com.

ISBN 0-7880-1808-6   PRINTED IN U.S.A.

Introduction

As a church teacher of children, are there times when you need to:
- add a little pizzazz and fun to introduce or review a Bible story or teaching?
- find a different way to review the memory work?
- fill extra time before the bell rings?
- help wiggly children find a way to use up their energy?

Are there moments when you must come up with something to do, but your mind is a blank (or as one teacher put it, you "run out of soap")?

Here are fresh ways to tell Bible stories, review memory work, teach the Bible, or fill extra time, while invigorating children by allowing them to participate. There are games, both quiet and active; paper and pencil activities; and board games. These are not just for one-time use but may be utilized again and again. Young children love doing familiar things, so the repetition will suit them just fine.

All the games and activities are easy to learn and require minimal materials and preparation. If you get the "props" ready ahead of time, you can keep them in a church cabinet for instant use. Memorize the rhymes and songs and become familiar with the game instructions. Then you will be ready for that special moment when you need a little extra "soap."

May God bless you in your special task and splendid privilege of teaching children God's wonderful Word.

Table Of Contents

I. Bible Story Activities

II. Action Games

III. Memory Work Review Games

IV. Paper And Pencil Activities

V. Board Games

1. Daniel In The Lions' Den
(Daniel 6)

Purpose
To review the story of Daniel and the lions with three different games.

Materials Needed
Photocopies of the sheet of pictures on page 9, construction paper, glue, envelopes.

Preparation
Duplicate four sheets of cards for each six players. Measure and cut 4x4 1/2-inch pieces of construction paper, one for each picture. Cut the pictures apart and glue to the construction paper pieces. Put each set into an envelope.

Game One: Find The Answer

Preparation
1. Use two sets of picture cards. Tell the story of Daniel and the lions. Show the pictures from one set of cards, telling what they represent:

1. King Darius	3. Bad Rulers	5. Roaring lions
2. Daniel	4. Daniel praying	6. Lions with mouths shut

2. After the story, lay one set of pictures on a table, face up.

Play The Game
1. Divide the players into two teams, seated in two lines of chairs, facing the table. As the players bring cards to you, keep the teams' cards separate.

2. Ask a question and name a player from each team. They run to the table, choose a picture, and bring it to you. If a player has the right picture, place it in his team's pile. If it is wrong, he must return it to the table and continue to look until one player finds the card. The two players are then seated, and you call the next question, etc.

3. After asking the first six questions, place the second set of cards on the table and ask the last six questions. Then count the cards earned by each team to see which one has the most.

Questions
1. Who was the king over all the land? (*King Darius*)
2. What good man did the king make ruler next to him? (*Daniel*)
3. What men hated Daniel? (*Bad rulers*)
4. The bad rulers got the king to sign a paper. It said that all people should pray only to the king. If someone broke the rule, where would he be put? (*Roaring lions*)
5. What did Daniel do about the king's rule? (*Daniel praying*)
6. What did God do for Daniel in the lions' den? (*Lions with shut mouths*)

7. Who came the next morning to see if Daniel was alive? (*King Darius*)

8. Who was brought out of the lions' den alive? (*Daniel*)

9. What did Daniel say God had done for him? (*Lions with shut mouths*)

10. Who was punished by the king? (*Bad rulers*)

11. Where were the bad rulers put? (*Lions' den*)

12. The king ruled that all people should pray only to God. What did Daniel do three times a day? (*Daniel praying*)

Game Two: Match Your Picture

Preparation

Four copies of one picture are needed for each player. One player will have four of #1, another, four of #2, etc. If there are more than six children, two or more players will have four of #1, etc.

Play The Game

1. Seat the players in a circle, around a table or on the floor. Give each child one picture card, using all the cards from one set and as many as needed from another set or sets. Each player puts his card in front of him, face up. Shuffle the remaining cards and put them in a pile in the center of the circle, face down.

2. Each player draws one card from the pile. If it matches his card, he puts it on top of his first card and draws again.

3. When each player has a card in his hand, play a verse of a recorded Sunday school song or sing a verse of a familiar children's church song. The players pass the cards around the circle, clockwise, until the last note/word is played/sung. Then, if they hold a card which matches, they put it on top of their pile and draw another card. When a player has all four cards, he drops out of the game. Continue until all players have all four cards.

Game Three: Hunt Your Matching Pictures

Preparation

Use four cards of one number for each player. While players close their eyes, hide three pictures per player in the room at or below child's-eye level.

Play The Game

1. Give each player one of the pictures that was not hidden. At a signal, all players hunt for three more copies of their pictures. Then they are seated.

2. When all players are seated, let each child show his picture and tell something about it.

1

2

3

4

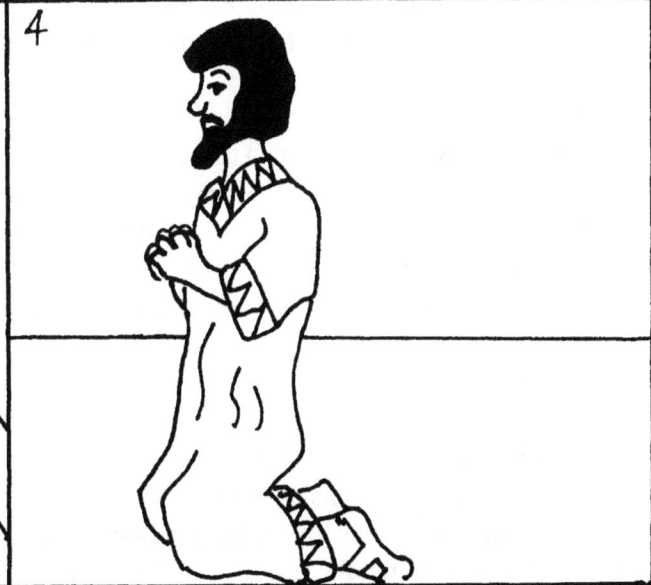

5

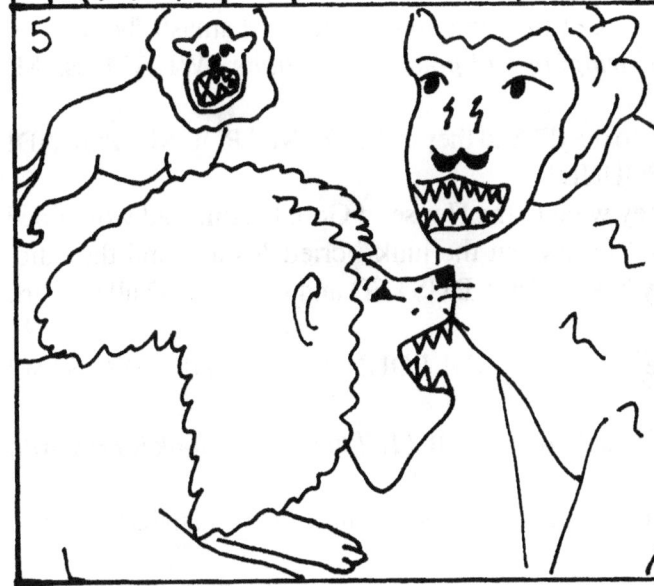

6

9

2. A Lost Treasure Found
(2 Kings 23-24; 2 Chronicles 34-35)

Purpose

To tell and act out the story of King Josiah and the lost Book found in the temple.

Materials Needed

Two pieces each of 8x12-inch brown and white construction paper, four 14-inch dowel sticks or drinking straws, glue, two rubber bands.

Preparation

Make two scrolls. Glue the white paper to the brown. Print a Bible verse on each scroll. With the white paper inside, roll each end around a stick or straw and glue in place. When dry, roll up the paper on the left stick. Fasten each roll with a rubber band. Hide one scroll in the room.

Introduction

Long, long ago, God told men to write the words of our Bible. Their books, called *scrolls*, were not like ours. They looked like this. (*Hold up the second scroll.*) People made scrolls from animal skins. They scraped the skins until they were very clean. Then they wrote God's words on the scroll. (*Open the scroll.*) Most people only heard the words of God's Book when someone read them at the House of God.

Let's pretend to be some people who lived long ago. While I tell the story, do what I do to act out the story.

A Lost Treasure Found

Josiah became the king of Israel when he was only eight years old. Josiah loved God. When he grew older, he said, "I want to make God happy. I will do what He wants me to do."

Josiah saw idols everywhere. People bowed down and prayed to them instead of God. "Idols are made of stone or wood or metal," said Josiah. "They are not God. We must destroy them."

Josiah and his men took heavy axes and hammers. "Cut the idols into pieces and smash them," said Josiah. And they did. WHAM! BAM! SMASH! (*Do swinging and pounding motions.*) WHAM! BAM! SMASH!

When the idols were broken, Josiah said, "Beat them to dust!" And they did. POUND! POUND! POUND! (*Pound your fist on your hand.*) POUND! POUND! POUND!

"Now we must clean God's house," said Josiah. They went to the House of God. No one had worshiped God there for a long time. They saw junk all around. "Throw out the junk," cried Josiah. And they did. WHISH! WHISH! WHIZZ! (*Throwing motions.*) They SWEPT and DUSTED and CLEANED all the dirt. (*Sweeping and dusting motions.*)

"Fix all the broken places," said Josiah. And they did. POUND! POUND! POUND! SAW! SAW! SAW! (*Pound and saw.*)

"Look! Look what I have found!" cried the priest. He held up a scroll. (*Tell the class to look for a scroll, hidden in the room. After someone finds it, unroll it.*)

The priest opened the old, old scroll and looked at it. A man took the scroll to King Josiah. "We have found the Book of God!" he cried.

"Read it to me," said Josiah. "I have never heard the words of God." When he heard the words, Josiah was very SAD. (*Wipe away tears.*) "Our people have not obeyed God for many years," he said. He called the people together. They listened to God's Book. "I will obey God's words," said Josiah. "Will you?"

"Yes, yes!" promised the people. They helped King Josiah smash more idols. WHAM! BAM! SMASH! They pounded them to dust. POUND! POUND! POUND! At last all the idols were gone.

The people came to the beautiful, clean House of God. They worshiped God and had a special feast. They worshiped God and ate good food. YUM! YUM! YUM! (*Pretend to eat.*) "It is good to do what God tells us," they said. "We are very happy now." And God was happy, too.

3. David, The Shepherd Boy
(1 Kings 16:11-12; 17:34-37)

Purpose

To act out the story of young David as a shepherd.

Materials Needed

None.

Preparation

In this story, you and the class will act out the time when a lion and a bear stole sheep from David, and he killed them. Caution the children that they must not grab or hurt each other. The lion and bear must only touch a child who is a sheep, and David only touches the lion and the bear when he "kills" them. When the children first act out this story, you will have to stop often and tell them what to do; but they will enjoy doing the story other times. Soon they will know what to do without being told.

Choose one child to be David, one to be a lion, and one to be a bear. The remaining children will be the sheep. Choose a corner of the room for the sheep barn. At the beginning of the story, David and the sheep stand there. The opposite end of the room will be the pasture. The lion and the bear hide near it. If possible, one adult should read the story, while another adult helps the children do the actions.

Tell The Story With Actions

David, The Shepherd Boy

"Come, sheep, we must go out to the pasture," said David, the shepherd boy. (*He begins to walk slowly toward the other side of the room, with the sheep following him on hands and knees, if possible.*) BAA, BAA! said the sheep. (*They baa as they go along.*)

At last, David brought the sheep to a fine pasture. (*They reach the other side of the room.*) "Here is soft, green grass to eat," said David. The sheep ATE the grass. CHOMP, CHOMP! (*The sheep pretend to eat.*) The sheep were very hungry. They ate and ate the good, sweet grass. CHOMP, CHOMP, CHOMP!

"Are you thirsty?" David asked after a while. "Come, sheep. I will take you to a brook. You can get a cool drink of water." (*David walks to a nearby spot, with the sheep following him.*) BAA, BAA! said the sheep. (*They baa.*) The sheep LAPPED the water with their tongues. LAP, LAP, LAP. (*The sheep drink.*) The water was good!

"It is getting hot," said David. "Let's go to a shady place where you can rest." (*David leads the sheep to another spot. The sheep lie down. David sits down.*) David took out his harp and played sweet music. (*He pretends to strum on the strings.*) The sheep went to sleep. Pretty soon, David fell asleep, too. (*They all lie down and close their eyes.*)

The lion was not sleeping. Quietly, he CREPT UP on the sheep. (*The lion creeps up and touches a sheep, who must crawl away with him.*) BAA, BAA! calls the sheep. (*The sheep baas loudly.*)

David WOKE UP. He RAN after the lion and TOOK the sheep from him. (*David awakes, runs after the lion and touches the sheep, who returns to the other sheep.*)

AARUGHA! the lion ROARED. (*The lion roars.*) He RAN after David, and David KILLED the lion! (*He touches the lion's shoulder, and the lion lies down, "dead." David goes back to the sheep.*)

(*Repeat the actions of going to the pasture, etc. if you wish.*) Another day, when the sheep and David were resting, a bear SNEAKED up. (*The bear crawls up and touches a sheep, who follows him.*) David RAN after the bear. He TOOK the sheep away from him, and he KILLED the bear! (*Repeat the actions as with the lion. David returns to the sheep.*)

"Thank you, God," said David. (*He folds his hands in prayer.*) "Thank you for helping me take care of the sheep. Thank you for being my Shepherd and taking care of me."

I. Bible Study Activities

4. The Snake On A Pole
(Numbers 21:4-8)

Purpose
To review the story of the snakes in the wilderness.

Materials Needed
Photocopies of the sheet of pictures on page 16, construction paper, glue, envelopes.

Preparation
These games use picture cards, as in "Daniel In The Lion's Den," page 7. Follow the directions there for preparing the cards.

Game One: Find The Answer

Cards Needed
Two sets of the picture cards.

Preparation
Before playing the game, tell the story of the snakes in the wilderness. Then show the pictures from one set of cards. Be sure that the children know what each picture is about:

1. Manna and water from the rock
2. Israelites grumbling to Moses
3. Snakes
4. Boy, bitten by a snake
5. Brass snake on a pole
6. People looking at the snake

After telling the story, lay one set of pictures on a table, face up.

Play The Game
Follow the rules as in Game One of "Daniel In The Lions' Den," page 7, except that the same questions will be used for the first and second set of cards laid on the table.

Questions
1. When the Israelites were in the hot desert, what did God give them to eat and drink? (*Manna and water from a rock*)
2. What did the people do about the good things God gave them? (*People grumbling to Moses*)
3. What did God send to punish the Israelites? (*Snakes*)
4. What did the snakes do? (*Boy, bitten by a snake*)
5. The people were sorry for grumbling. They told Moses to ask God to help them. What did God tell Moses to do? (*Brass snake on a pole*)
6. Moses told the people to look at the snake on the pole, and God would heal them. What did most of the people do? (*People looking at the snake*)

Lay out the second set of cards and repeat the same questions as you play the game again. Count the cards the two teams have given you in both games to determine the winner.

Game Two: Match Your Picture

Cards Needed

Four copies of one picture for each player, as in Game Two of "Daniel In The Lions' Den," page 8.

Play The Game

Play by the directions for Game Two of "Daniel In The Lions' Den." Use the following lines:

The Israelites, they grumbled;
    So God sent snakes to bite.
If they saw the snake of brass,
    God made them quite all right!

Game Three: Hunt Your Matching Pictures

Use the same number of cards and play by the directions as in Game Three of "Daniel In The Lions' Den," page 8.

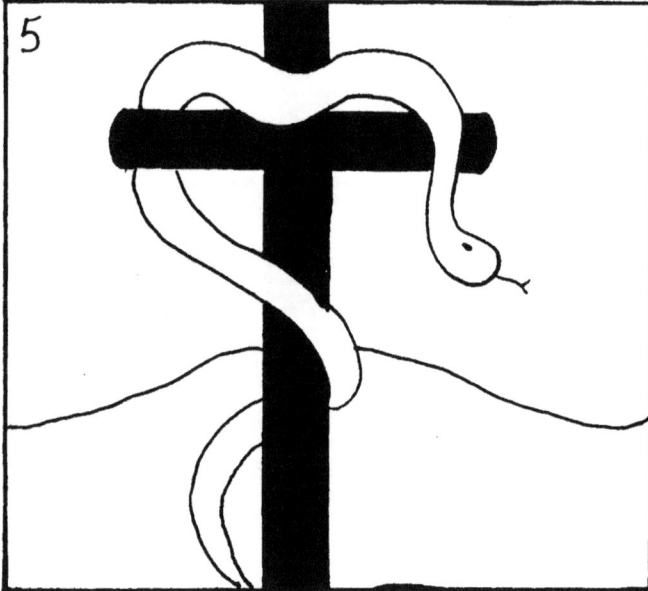

5. The Days Of Creation
(Genesis 1)

Purpose

To review the story of creation.

Materials Needed

Enough photocopies of the picture sheet on page 19 so that each child will have one of the pictures.

Preparation

Glue the picture sheets to construction paper and cut the pictures apart.

Game One: Which Day?

Play The Game

1. Seat the children in a circle. Hold up each picture card and talk about what it represents. Give each child a card. For younger children, name the picture again as you give it.

2. Name a day of creation and what God did on that day. (See the list below.) The child holding that picture should stand. Repeat, as needed, until the children can do it well.

Day of Creation	Event
First Day	Light (day and night)
Second Day	Sky and water
Third Day	Sea and earth; trees and plants
Fourth Day	Sun, moon, and stars
Fifth Day	Fish and birds
Sixth Day	Animals and man
Seventh Day	God rested

3. Tell the following story and pause after each capitalized word. The child or children holding the correct card will stand. If a child makes a mistake, have him sit down until his turn comes. All other children, after standing, will remain standing throughout the story.

When God Created

In the beginning, God created the heaven and the earth. On the first day of creation, God said, "Let there be light, and there was LIGHT ... God called the light "day" and the darkness "night."

On the second day, God divided the waters above from the waters beneath, and then there was SKY AND WATER ...

On the third day, God said, "Let the seas gather together into oceans, and let the dry land appear." So there was SEA AND EARTH ... God made TREES AND PLANTS ... to spring up on the earth, also. And God said that it was good.

On the fourth day, God said, "Let the lights appear in the sky in the day and in the night." The SUN, MOON, AND STARS ... shone in the night. And God said that it was good.

17

On the fifth day, God made FISH ... to live in the waters. He made BIRDS ... to fly in the sky or to live on the land. And God said that it was good.

On the sixth day, God made ANIMALS ... Also, on the sixth day, God made MAN ... and God said that it was good.

On the seventh day, God RESTED.... (*All children sit.*)

4. Take up the cards, mix them up, and give them out again. Repeat the story and its actions as often as you wish.

Game Two: Days Of Creation Review

Play The Game

1. After doing the above activity, review the days of creation with this game. Give each child one card. Do not give out the card that says "rest."

2. Place chairs in a circle, facing out, one less than the number of players. All the players are seated, except one, who follows behind you as you walk around the circle. In random order, call out the name of a day and its picture. (First Day — Light, etc.). The player who holds the picture named begins to follow you. Continue walking, until you say, "Seventh Day — God rested." Then all the players scramble for a chair.

3. The player who has no chair follows you as you begin again. This time, give each player a different card.

Rest

6. The Boy Jesus Goes To The Temple
(Luke 2:41-52)

Purpose

To act out the story of Jesus going to the temple.

Materials Needed

Photocopies of the puppet figures on page 22, empty toilet tissue rolls, stapler, crayons, glue.

Preparation

Duplicate enough puppet figures so that half of the children (Group One) will have the figure of Jesus, and half (Group Two) will have Mary and Joseph. Ahead of time, prepare an extra set to be used by two adults. Cut out the figures on the outer lines. For each puppet, provide a flattened toilet tissue roll.

Make The Puppets

Give out the puppet figures and the tissue rolls to the children. They will color their puppet and glue it to the roll, lengthwise. Their four fingers should fit snugly inside the end of the roll. If not, staple the sides of the roll to fit.

Act Out The Story

Choose one side of the room to be Nazareth, Jesus' home town. Place the children there, with Group One on the right and Group Two on the left. All face the opposite side of the room, which will be the temple in Jerusalem. One adult should stand with each group, holding the proper puppet and leading the group in the actions called for. Hold up the puppet indicated by the words in capital letters and follow other directions as stated.

Say, *Let's imagine what it was like long ago when Jesus was a twelve-year-old boy.*

A Very Special Trip

Flowers bloomed and birds sang in Nazareth. It was springtime. "Tomorrow we start on our trip to Jerusalem," said Joseph. "Everything is packed and ready. Tonight we must go to bed early to get plenty of sleep."

MARY and JOSEPH lay down on their mats and went to sleep (*place puppet in a horizontal position, face up*). JESUS lay down, too (*lay puppet down*). He was too excited to sleep. What a fine time they would have in Jerusalem! He was twelve now, so he could go into the temple with Joseph. He could hardly wait!

Morning came. While it was still dark, MARY and JOSEPH got up (*hold puppet up*). They woke up JESUS (*hold him up*). Soon they were walking down the road to Jerusalem (*both groups slowly walk toward the other side of the room*). Many other people were walking, also. It was a long, long trip. Step, step, step! They walked mile after mile.

At noontime, everyone stopped to eat (*stop walking*). Mary got out their food. "Come, Jesus," she called. "It is time to eat." (*Both groups sit down in one circle.*) Soon they walked on again (*do so*). Step, step, step!

As the sun went down, they stopped for the night. MARY and JOSEPH and JESUS wrapped themselves in their coats and lay down on the ground (*lay puppets down as before*). Jesus looked up at the stars, twinkling in the sky. Then he fell fast asleep.

After two or three days of walking, they climbed a hill. There was Jerusalem! (*Walk to the temple area.*) Everyone took part in the big Passover Feast. They stayed for several days. Then it was time to go home. MARY and JOSEPH started out with the big crowd of people (*Group Two walks away*).

JESUS didn't notice they were leaving (*Group One stays in the temple area*). Jesus loved to be in the temple. It was the house of His Father, God.

MARY AND JOSEPH thought Jesus was in the crowd of people. They walked on through the day — step, step, step (*slowly walk toward the opposite side of the room*). Evening came. As they stopped to camp for the night, they looked for Jesus. "Have you seen Jesus?" they asked all around. No one had seen him. Jesus was not there!

Early the next morning, MARY and JOSEPH hurried back to Jerusalem (*they walk fast*). When they got to the city, they looked for Jesus (*move puppets near the temple area but not inside it*). They looked all over the city (*walk them all around, stopping to ask questions*).

After two days, MARY and JOSEPH went to the temple (*have them do so*). There was JESUS! He was listening to the teachers. He was asking them questions. The teachers were surprised that such a young boy could talk so wisely.

"We have been very worried, Son," said Mary. "We have been looking everywhere for you."

"Why were you looking for me?" asked Jesus. "Didn't you know I had to be in my Father's house?"

JESUS walked home with MARY and JOSEPH (*they walk to the other side of the room*). Jesus obeyed them, and he was always good and kind. He grew tall and strong. Mary and Joseph were pleased with him. And so was his heavenly Father, God.

Cut
here

22

1. Which One?

Purpose

To review Bible stories. Five examples are given. Make up words and actions for playing the game with other Bible stories.

Materials Needed

None.

Play The Game

1. Teach the rhyme and the motions by repeating them with the children several times.

2. Choose one child to be "It." He stands a few feet in front of the other players, with his back toward them.

3. Repeat the rhyme, doing the motions. At the end, quietly indicate to the children which position to hold. "It" guesses which it is. If he is correct, he chooses a player to take his place. If not, he continues until he guesses correctly.

Tall Or Small?

(David and Goliath)

I'm Goliath — big and TALL; (*Stand tall.*)
    Now I'm David — very SMALL. (*Stoop down.*)
TALL or SMALL; TALL or SMALL —
    Which one am I now?

Blind Or Seeing?

(Jesus Heals the Blind Man)

I'm the man who was born BLIND; (*Hold hands over eyes.*)
    Jesus came, and now I SEE! (*Remove hands; open eyes.*)
BLIND or SEEING; BLIND or SEEING —
    Which way am I now?

Boat Or Fish?

(Jonah)

I am Jonah in the BOAT; (*Cup hands, like a boat.*)
    Now I'm swallowed by the FISH. (*Close left hand over fingers of right hand.*)
BOAT or FISH; BOAT or FISH —
    Which place am I now?

Waves Or Calm?

(Jesus Calms the Storm)

We're the WAVES upon the sea; (*Make big waves with hands.*)
    Now we're CALM as we can be. (*Hold extended hands still.*)
WAVES or CALM; WAVES or CALM —
    Which way are we now?

Jail Or Free?

(Peter's Escape from Prison)

I am Peter in the JAIL; (*Right index finger inside left hand.*)
    Now I'm FREE outside the gate. (*Pull out finger; hold it up.*)
JAIL or FREE; JAIL or FREE —
    Which place am I now?

2. Let's Go Fishing

Purpose

To review a Bible story that has pictures to illustrate it.

Materials Needed

Flashcards or other pictures of any Bible story, a large box or tub, a short pole or stick, string, a spring clothespin, a few pieces of red paper, a snack for each pupil (a sack of crackers, raisins, "o" cereal, or other healthful, dry snacks).

Preparation

Tie the string on the end of the pole. Securely fasten a clothespin to the other end of the string. Put the box or tub on a table and place the pictures and red papers inside.

Play The Game

1. An adult stands behind the box or tub. Each child, in turn, throws the line into it. The adult pins a card to the clothespin and gives the line a tug. The child pulls in the "fish." He must then tell something about the picture. If he can, he receives his snack and sits down to eat it. If he can't tell anything about the picture, he must try again when the others have received their snacks. (The second time, prompt a child if he still has problems.)

2. Occasionally, tie on a red paper instead of a picture. The child may then receive a snack without saying anything.

3. Let the children fish again with the same pictures, but with no snacks, if they want to fish again.

3. Put The Star In The Sky
(Matthew 2)

Purpose

To review the story of the wise men.

Materials Needed

A copy of the picture of the house (page 27), yellow construction paper, masking tape, a blindfold.

Preparation

Duplicate the picture of the house and color it. Using the star as a pattern, cut from yellow paper enough stars for each child to have one. Tape the picture of the house on a wall, low enough for every child to reach it easily. Place a small piece of tape to each star.

Play The Game

1. Blindfold one player at a time. Turn him around three times and face him in the direction of the house. He will try to tape the star directly above the house. The winner is the one whose star is nearest to the right place.

4. Resurrection Relay
(Matthew 28:1-10)

Purpose

To review the story of Jesus' resurrection.

Materials Needed

None.

Preparation

Before playing the game the first time, tell the story of the women who came to the tomb and heard the angel's message. Then teach the class to say, "Jesus is not here. He is alive."

Play The Game

1. Divide the players into two teams. Help them form two parallel lines, facing forward. Several feet in front of the lines, place two chairs, which each represent Jesus' tomb. Choose a player from each line to stand by his team's "tomb" and be an "angel."

2. At a signal, the first player in each line runs to his tomb. The angel says, "Jesus is not here. He is alive." The player then becomes the angel, and the former angel runs back to the line, taps the next player, and goes to the back of the line. The second player goes to the tomb, etc., until all players have repeated the message. If you wish to choose a winner, it would be the team which finishes first.

Variation

If most of your children are not ready for team play, have them form one line. They may take turns going to the tomb, receiving the message, and being the angel.

5. My Gifts To The Church

Purpose

To help children learn that their offerings help to buy the things they and/or their teachers use in church.

Materials Needed

Objects in your classroom and a musical instrument or a tape player with a musical cassette tape.

Preparation

Place around the room, in easy reach of the children, some teaching tools which you use in your class. These could include pictures, books, Bibles, take-home papers, toys, crayons, etc.

Play The Game

1. While music is being played, the children march around the room wherever they wish. When the music stops, each child must touch something that is used in class.

2. Ask two or three children to say what they are touching and how it is used. They may hold it up if it is small. Repeat the music and marching several times, until each child has participated.

For Discussion

When the children are seated, talk about the items again. Say, *Most of these items were bought. Who gave the money? Did your offerings help to buy them? When you give to church, you are giving to Jesus. Do you think He is happy when you help buy things we can use in church?*

6. David's Stone

(1 Samuel 17)

Purpose

To review the story of David and Goliath.

Materials Needed

A small, smooth stone and a blindfold (optional).

Preparation

Repeat the rhyme below several times with the children until they are familiar with it. During the game, lead them each time they say it.

Play The Game

1. Choose one player to be "It" and blindfold him (or he may close his eyes). Seat the other players in a circle around "It." Give one player the stone. As the rhyme is repeated, the players pass the stone from one to the other. When the last word of the rhyme is said, the player holding the stone hides it inside his fist. He and all other players then hold out their fists.

2. "It" removes the blindfold or opens his eyes. He taps the fist where he thinks the stone is hidden. If he is wrong, he may try two more times. If he is still wrong, he is "It" again. If he finds the stone, the player holding it becomes "It."

> David, David threw a stone —
> Hit Goliath in the head;
> Old Goliath, he fell down;
> The giant man was dead!

7. Pick A Picture

Purpose

To use with the quiz, "Bible People Match-Up."

Materials Needed

Copies of the pictures of Bible things and animals on pages 33 and 34, construction paper, glue.

Preparation

Make two photocopies of each page of Bible things and animals. (Each page is one set.) Glue each set to a different color of construction paper. Cut the pictures apart, keeping the sets separate.

Play The Game

1. Divide the players into two teams. Seat the players of each team together. On a nearby table, place a set of pictures, face up, on either end of the table. Show each team where their set of pictures is.

2. Questions 1-12 go with Picture Set #1, and questions 13-24 go with Picture Set #2. Ask the first question. The first player of each team goes to his team's pictures, chooses the picture which he thinks answers the question, and brings it to you. If a player has a correct picture, he keeps it. If his picture is incorrect, he returns it to the table and sits down.

3. Continue until all questions have been answered. (The players may have to take more than one turn.) Count the picture cards earned by each team to determine a winner.

4. When the pupils are familiar with the questions and pictures, place both sets of pictures on the table for each team and use all the questions.

Bible People Match-Up

(To use with the quiz game, "Pick A Picture")

1. What did Zaccheus climb up to see Jesus? (*A tree*)
2. What kind of creatures fed Elijah during a famine? (*Ravens*)
3. What kind of animals did David look after when he was a boy? (*Sheep*)
4. Daniel was thrown into a den of what kind of animals? (*Lions*)
5. What did Jesus use to feed five thousand people? (*Five loaves and two fishes*)
6. What did the wise men follow to see Jesus? (*A star*)
7. What did Noah and his family live in during the flood? (*An ark*)
8. What did Mary use for Baby Jesus' bed? (*A manger*)
9. What strange thing did Peter walk on? (*Water*)
10. What swallowed Jonah? (*A whale*)
11. What creature did Satan use when he tempted Eve? (*A serpent*)
12. What was Jesus nailed to when he died? (*A cross*)
13. Who told the shepherds about Baby Jesus? (*An angel*)
14. What did Moses' mother put him in to save his life? (*A basket*)
15. What did Joseph see that reached from earth to heaven, with angels on it? (*A ladder*)
16. What did God put in the sky as a promise to Noah there would never be another world flood? (*A rainbow*)
17. What special thing did Jacob give Joseph to wear? (*A coat of many colors*)

18. On what did God write the Ten Commandments? (*Tablets of stone*)

19. What were Jesus and the disciples riding in when a terrible storm came? (*A boat*)

20. What weapon did David use against Goliath? (*A sling and a stone*)

21. What did Abraham live in? (*A tent*)

22. What musical instrument did David play? (*A harp*)

23. What animal did God cause to talk? (*A donkey*)

24. What did God put in the sky to give us light in the day? (*The sun*)

Picture Set #1

33

Picture Set #2

34

8. Catching Fish

Purpose

To use with the quiz, "Fish Stories In The Bible," or with other quizzes or memory work.

Materials Needed

A 21x28-inch posterboard, nylon netting, two colors of construction paper, glue, crayons or paints (optional).

Preparation

On the posterboard, make an enlarged drawing of the fishing scene on page 37. Color it, if you wish. Cut a 10x16 inch piece of nylon netting. Fold it in half, crosswise, and sew the two sides together, making a bag, 8x10 inches. Glue one side of the bag's top below the children's hands. From the fish pattern, cut twenty to thirty or more fish from construction paper, half of one color and half of another. Put the fish in an open box.

Play The Game

1. Divide the players into two teams, and state each team's color. Seat the players of each team together. The teams will answer questions alternately.

2. Give the statement and question. A player must choose which answer is right. If correct, the player puts a fish of his team's color in the fishing net. If needed, repeat the questions to let all players participate at least once.

3. Count the fish to find the winning team. If you wish, the contest may continue for several weeks, using other quizzes and/or memory work before the fish are counted.

Fish Stories In The Bible
(To be used with the quiz game, "Catching Fish")

1. In the first of the ten plagues God sent on Egypt, the fish in the rivers died. Was it because God turned the waters to INK or BLOOD? (*Blood.* Exodus 7:20-21)

2. Jonah got on a ship and sailed away. He wanted to run from someone. Was it GOD or the POLICE? (*God.* Jonah 1:3)

3. God sent a storm that nearly broke up the ship where Jonah was. Jonah told the sailors to do something. Was it to THROW HIM OVERBOARD or TIE HIM TO THE SHIP'S MAST? (*Throw him overboard.* Jonah 1:12)

4. A great fish swallowed Jonah. Was he in its stomach for THREE DAYS or THREE MINUTES? (*Days.* Jonah 1:17)

5. Jonah did something inside the fish. Did he YELL AT GOD or PRAY? (*Pray.* Jonah 2:7)

6. When the fish spit Jonah up on dry land, Jonah went somewhere right away. Was it to JERUSALEM TO PRAY or to NINEVEH TO PREACH? (*Nineveh to preach.* Jonah 3:3)

7. Jonah preached in Nineveh, as God told him to do. What did the people there do — THROW JONAH OUT OF TOWN or REPENT OF THEIR SINS? (*Repent of their sins.* John 3:5)

8. Jesus told Peter to catch a fish with a hook, and he would find a piece of money in its mouth. Was it to PAY A TAX or to BUY A TOY? (*Pay a tax.* Matthew 17:27)

9. One day Jesus saw Peter and Andrew by the sea, and he told them to follow him. What were they doing by the sea — EATING THEIR LUNCH or CASTING A NET INTO THE SEA? (*Casting a net.* Matthew 4:16)

10. Jesus fed 5,000 people with a boy's lunch. There were five loaves in the lunch. Were there TWO FISH or A MILLION FISH? (*Two fish.* John 6:8)

11. One time Peter and some other disciples went fishing, but they caught nothing. Did they fish ONE HOUR or ALL NIGHT? (*All night.* John 21:3)

12. In the morning, Jesus stood on the shore. Did he tell them to QUIT FISHING or CAST THEIR NET IN THE WATER AGAIN? (*Cast their net.* John 21:6)

13. The disciples cast their net and caught something. Was it ONE GREAT BIG FISH or 153 BIG FISH? (*153 fish.* John 21:11)

14. When the disciples came to shore, Jesus had breakfast for them. Was it BREAD AND FISH or JELLO AND CAKE? (*Bread and fish.* John 21:13)

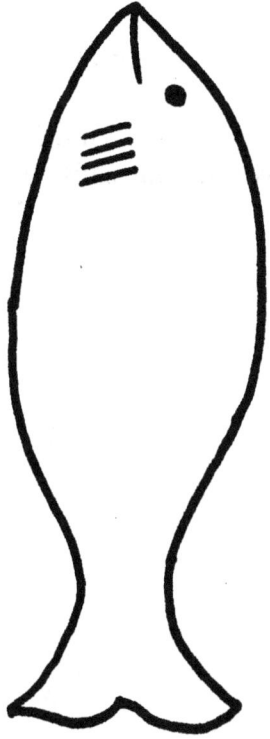

9. Skunk!

(Genesis 2:19)

Purpose

To teach that God made the animals, and Adam named them.

Materials Needed

None.

Play The Game

1. Read Genesis 2:19. Give each child the name of an animal that makes a sound. Be sure each one knows the proper sound.

2. Arrange chairs in a large circle, one less chair than players. Choose one child to be Adam. (While he is playing Adam, he will not use his animal name.) He walks around inside the circle of chairs and calls out the names of animals, one at a time. The children who play those animals follow him, making the animals' sounds, until Adam calls out, "Skunk!"

3. Adam and the animals scramble for chairs, holding their noses. They sit down. The one who does not have a chair plays the next Adam.

10. Sit-Down Hide-and-Seek

Purpose

To review a Bible story by helping pupils visualize an indoor or outdoor scene in it.

Materials Needed

None.

Play The Game

1. Use the day's Bible story or briefly review another story. Let the players name places in the story's location where they might "hide." For instance, in the story of Jesus' birth in the stable, the places could be: behind the manger, under the cattle's straw, behind a cow or sheep, behind Joseph, Mary, or a shepherd, and in a dark corner of the stable.

2. Players sit in a circle in chairs or on the floor. Choose one player to be "It," who then says, "I am hiding in the stable. Where am I?" The players take turns guessing, and the one who "finds" "It" will be the next "It."

11. Sound Effects*

Purpose
To emphasize church attendance and being on time.

Materials Needed
None.

Before Playing
Divide the players into eight groups of one or more persons. Assign a sound effect to each group which they will make when a certain phrase is read. Review the sounds several times until each group is familiar with the sound to make. (Adults may help younger players.) Use the names of your own town and church for "your town" and "your church."

(Your town)	How do you do?
(Your church)	Ding-dong, ding-dong
Sunday school	Hooray!
Cars	Vroom! Vroom!
Slowpokes	Clump ... Clump ... Clump
First song	"Jesus Loves Me" (first line)
Second song	"Jesus Loves the Little Children" (first line)
Offering	Clink, clink, clink

Play The Game
Read the story, pausing after each capitalized phrase for the sound effect. Encourage enthusiastic sound effects.

When The Slowpokes Went To Sunday School
Once upon a time there was a fine town called (YOUR TOWN) ... In the town of (YOUR TOWN) ... was the (YOUR CHURCH) ... At the (YOUR CHURCH) ... every Sunday morning they had SUNDAY SCHOOL ... Many people from (YOUR TOWN) ... went to the SUNDAY SCHOOL ... at (YOUR CHURCH) ... Some early comers came in their CARS ... They hurried to be there early. Others walked, but they got there on time, too. But some — oh, for shame! — some were SLOWPOKES ... They started much too late and came much too slowly ... those SLOWPOKES ....

One Sunday morning at the SUNDAY SCHOOL ... of the (YOUR CHURCH) ... in (YOUR TOWN) ... they began right on time. The early comers who came in their CARS ... were there. Those who walked were there. They sang the FIRST SONG ... but the SLOWPOKES ... were not there. They sang the SECOND SONG.... Still, the SLOWPOKES ... had not arrived. Then they took the OFFERING ...

At last the SLOWPOKES ... came clumping in the door. When they realized how late they were, they said. "We have missed the FIRST SONG ... We have missed the SECOND SONG ... We have even missed the OFFERING ... We will not be SLOWPOKES ... any more. Next Sunday we will be on time."

So now in (YOUR TOWN) ... at the SUNDAY SCHOOL ... of the (YOUR CHURCH) ... everyone comes on time: those who come in CARS ... and those who walk. They all sing the FIRST SONG ... and the SECOND SONG ... and they give in the OFFERING ... And there are no SLOWPOKES ... at all!

*Originally published in *More Children's Church Time.*

1. Digging For Silver And Gold

Purpose

To review memory verses or other memory work.

Materials Needed

Yellow (representing gold) and gray (representing silver) construction paper and three medium-sized paper sacks.

Preparation

Cut 2" paper circles from construction paper — about two gray (silver) for each player and a total of five yellow (gold). Place all the circles in a sack and mix them up.

Before Playing The Game

Review the memory verse(s) or other memory work which the pupils will repeat in the game.

Read Proverbs 16:16. Say, *God's wisdom is found in the Bible. When you memorize it, you have something far better than gold or silver. The Bible tells you how to go to heaven, how to live right, and how to be happy. Gold and silver can't do that.*

Play The Game

1. Divide the players into two teams and give each team an empty paper sack.

2. An adult holds the sack containing the circles in front of the players, high enough that they can't see inside. The first player from Team One draws out a circle. If it is silver, the player repeats the memory work. If he is correct, he puts the circle in Team One's sack. If he is incorrect, he puts it in Team Two's sack. A gold circle is free, requiring no memory work. The first player on Team Two is next. Continue, alternating teams, until all players have had a turn or all circles are in the teams' sacks.

3. To determine the winner, count the circles in each sack. Silver circles get one point each and gold circles get two.

2. Say To Stay

Purpose

To review memory verses or other memory work.

Materials Needed

(Optional) A piano or a tape recorder and a music tape.

Before Playing The Game

Review the memory verse(s) or other memory work to use in the game.

Play The Game

1. Place all the chairs in a large circle, facing outside, one less chair than players.

2. The players line up in a circle outside the chairs. Play music on the piano or the tape recorder. (If you don't have either, an adult can sing or say, "Go.") The players march around the circle. When the music stops (or the adult says, "Stop!"), the players sit down in the chairs.

3. The player who has no chair must recite the memory verse(s) to stay in the game. If he cannot do so correctly, he sits or stands away from the circle, and one chair is removed. Continue as long as you wish or until only one player remains.

3. Stars In Your Crown

Purpose

To review the memory verses for one month.

Materials Needed

Yellow construction paper, gummed stars, a stapler, masking tape.

Preparation

For each child, cut one sheet of 9x12-inch yellow paper in two pieces — one 6x12 inches and the other 3x12 inches. Cut points on the larger piece, like a crown. Staple the two pieces together, lengthwise, on one end. Measure each child's crown around his head so that it fits snugly, remove, and staple the other two ends. Write the child's name inside his crown.

Cut four stars from construction paper, about six inches wide. Number the stars 1 to 4. Tape them to a wall and place a chair underneath each star.

Play The Game

1. After the first Sunday's memory verse is taught, the children will take turns sitting on the chair under star #1 and repeating the verse. On the second Sunday, they will sit under the second star, etc.

2. Each Sunday, review the verses learned thus far by placing your hand on the correct chair and having the class repeat that verse.

3. On the fourth Sunday, let the children wear their crowns and take turns sitting in each chair and trying to say its verse. Put one star in the child's crown for each verse he says correctly. If a child cannot say a verse the first time, let him try again after the other children have finished.

4. Wastebasket Toss

Purpose

To review a memory verse or other memory work.

Materials Needed

A wastebasket, a bean bag or other object that can be thrown.

Preparation

Review the memory verse or other memory work until the children are familiar with it. Place the basket near one wall of the room. About five feet away, mark a line on the floor with chalk or masking tape.

Play The Game

1. The players take turns tossing the bean bag. A player who puts the bag into the basket receives six points. If the bag falls to the floor with any part of it touching the basket, the score is two points. The score is doubled for any player who can repeat the memory work perfectly.

2. Players who fail to score may try again after all other players have had a turn. Those who get a score but cannot repeat the memory work may try to say it again. If they do, add to their score one-half of its value.

3. The players keep their scores and play again, until all of them can say the memory work. The one with the highest score wins.

Tell the players, *You tossed an object into a wastebasket. When you put God's Word in your mind, though, you store up very valuable treasure for your whole lifetime.* Read Psalm 119:72.

5. Secret Message Relay

Purpose

To review short memory verses.

Materials Needed

None.

Play The Game

1. First, review some memory verses which the class has learned.

2. Divide the class into two teams, with older and younger children on each. At one end of the room, line up the two teams, facing forward. An adult stands at the opposite end.

3. At a signal, the first two players run to the adult, who quietly says a memory verse to them. The players run back, quietly repeat the verse to the next one in their line, and sit down. Each player, when hearing the "secret message," turns and repeats it to the next in line. The last player in line runs and tags the adult. The two players repeat the verse out loud, with the one who tagged first saying it first.

4. To score, give three points to the team whose player tagged first and five points to either team whose player said the verse correctly. Keep the scores and play again, using other verses.

6. Capture A Clothespin

Purpose

To review memory verses for several weeks.

Materials Needed

About two dozen spring clothespins, red and blue paints or sheets of construction paper, two pieces of string (two feet long), a paint brush or scissors and glue, two containers to hold the clothespins.

Preparation

On the front side, paint half the clothespins blue and half of them red. Or cut small pieces of construction paper and glue them to the clothespins. Place all the clothespins of one color in one container. Securely fasten the two ends of each string to the classroom wall, low enough for the children to reach them.

Play The Game

1. Divide the class into the Blue Team and the Red Team. They will compete for several weeks. Give each team their container of clothespins. Each team may snap one clothespin on their line now.

2. Review the day's memory verse. Taking turns, one player from each team tries to repeat the verse. A player who says the verse correctly may snap one clothespin on his team's line. If a player makes a mistake, the other player captures a pin from that player's line and snaps it on his own line. Continue in the same way until all players have had a turn.

3. Give the teams one point for each clothespin on their line when all have participated. Keep a record of each team's weekly score. Remove the clothespins from the lines.

4. As you continue to play each week, use the verses from former weeks as well as the day's verse.

7. Which Disciple?

Purpose
To help pupils become familiar with the disciples' names.

Materials Needed
None.

Preparation
None.

Play The Game
1. Give each player the name of a disciple. For less than twelve players, use adults as disciples or call the name, with no one responding. Be sure to name Peter, Andrew, James, John, Matthew, and Judas. For more than twelve players, give some the same name.

The twelve disciples: PETER, ANDREW, JAMES, JOHN, PHILIP, THOMAS, MATTHEW, JAMES (THE SON OF ALPHAEUS), THADDEUS, SIMON, JUDAS, and BARTHOLOMEW.

2. When a disciple's name is called in the story, the player(s) with that name stand and remain standing until told to be seated. Further instructions may be given also.

Jesus' Twelve Disciples
One day Jesus walked by the Sea of Galilee. He saw two fishermen throwing nets into the sea. They were brothers. Their names were PETER and ANDREW. Jesus said to them, "Follow me, and I will make you fishers of men." At once, they left their nets and followed Jesus.

Soon Jesus came to two more brothers. They were sitting in a boat with their father, mending their nets. Their names were JAMES and JOHN. "Follow me," Jesus said, and they did.

Another day Jesus saw a man collecting taxes at a tax booth. His name was MATTHEW. "Follow me," Jesus told him. And Matthew left his booth and followed Jesus.

Jesus called other disciples, until he had seven more. They were PHILIP, THOMAS, JAMES (THE SON OF ALPHAEUS), THADDAEUS, SIMON, JUDAS, and BARTHOLOMEW. Twelve disciples followed Jesus and helped him in his work. (*March around the room once, with all disciples following you. Then they sit down.*)

Three disciples were very special to Jesus. They were PETER, JAMES, and JOHN. One day they went up into a mountain with Him and saw His looks change. His face shone like the sun, and His clothes were as white as the light. (*The three disciples sit down.*)

The disciple who turned Jesus over to His enemies was JUDAS. Later, Judas went out and hanged himself. (*Judas walks away and sits in a far corner.*) Then there were eleven disciples: PETER, ANDREW, JAMES, JOHN, MATTHEW, PHILIP, THOMAS, JAMES (THE SON OF ALPHAEUS), THADDAEUS, SIMON, and BARTHOLOMEW.

When Jesus was on trial, PETER was very frightened. He said he didn't know Jesus. (*Peter sits down.*) Peter was sorry, and he went out and cried and prayed. Jesus forgave him, and PETER was still a disciple. (*Peter stands up again. Then all disciples sit down.*)

Before Jesus went back to heaven, He told His disciples to go and preach the Gospel. And that is what they did — PETER, ANDREW, JAMES, JOHN, PHILIP, THOMAS, MATTHEW, JAMES (THE SON OF ALPHAEUS), THADDAEUS, SIMON, and BARTHOLOMEW.

8. Bible Book Upset

Purpose

To help children learn the names of the Bible books.

Materials Needed

None.

Preparation

Teach four books at a time in order, beginning with the New Testament. Repeat these book names over and over. Think of ways to vary this. Some suggestions:

1. Stand and repeat the names once. Sit down and repeat them. Do this several times.
2. March around the room, repeating a book name with each step.
3. Clap hands while saying the names.

Play The Game

1. Make a large circle of chairs, one less than the number of players. Choose a player to be "It," who stands in the center of the circle. Give each player the name of a Bible book which you are learning. At least three players must have the same name. (If your class is too small for that, use only three book names.)

2. To be sure all players know their names, call out the book names one at a time. The players who have that name stand and repeat the name.

3. An adult calls out the name of one Bible book. The players having that name must exchange chairs. The child who is "It" does not use his Bible name while he is "It." Instead, he tries to catch one of the players exchanging seats. If he does, that player becomes the new "It."

4. Occasionally, call out, "Bible book upset!" All the players must exchange chairs, with "It" trying to catch one.

1. How Many Children Did Hannah Have?

Give each child a copy of the page. Read the sentences. Have the class say the words where there are pictures and count the faces. Then each one circles that number on his page.

Hannah did not have any children. She was very (sad).

1. How many children did Hannah have?   2   0   3

Hannah  (prayed). She said, "Dear God, please give me a  (baby) boy.

I will let him work for you." God gave Hannah a  (baby) boy, named Samuel.

2. Now how many children did she have?   1   6   2

Hannah took  (Samuel) to the temple to work for God.

God gave Hannah more children. Then she had  (Samuel)

and      more.

3. How many children did Hannah have in all?   1   3   6.

2. Jesus Makes A Dead Girl Alive

A little girl was very sick. Her father came to Jesus. "Please come and make my girl well," he said. On the way, a man met them. "Your little girl is dead," the man told the father.

"Don't be afraid," Jesus said. "Only believe, and she will be well." Draw a path between the houses for Jesus to get to the door of the little girl's house.

In the house, Jesus said, "My child, get up!" She stood up, all well. Draw her picture and color the page.

IV. Paper And Pencil Activities

3. Happy Or Sad?

Draw glad ⌣ sad ⌢ or mad ⌇⌇⌇ mouths.

1. Baby Jesus was born. Mary and Joseph were

2. The shepherds and angels were

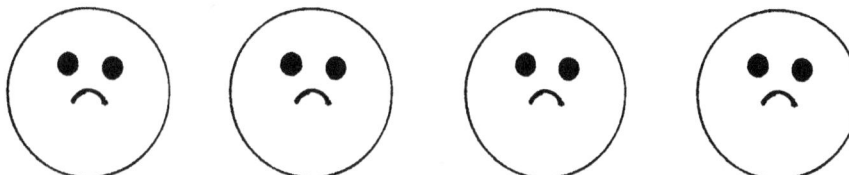

3. Jesus healed sick people. They were

4. Jesus taught about God. Many people were

5. Some bad people did not like Jesus' words. They were

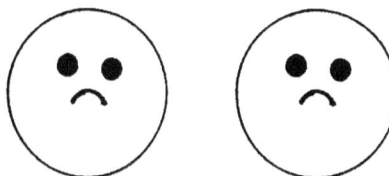

6. Jesus died on the cross. His friends were

7. Jesus came alive again. His friends were

8. Jesus loves me. I am

51

4. Jesus Died For Me

All people do bad things sometimes. They are called *sins*. Jesus never sinned. He took our place and died for our sins. Then He came alive again. Color the spaces with #1, brown; with #2, blue; and with #3, red. What did Jesus die on? A _____

3	3	3	3	3	3	3
3	2	2	1	2	2	3
3	2	1	1	1	2	3
3	2	2	1	2	2	3
3	2	2	1	2	2	3
3	3	3	3	3	3	3

(Trace the letters.) Jesus died for

5. How Many?

Fill each blank with the number to answer the question. Each letter under a blank line matches a number on the clock.

1. In how many days did God create the world?

2. How many Gods are there?

3. How many commandments did God give Moses?

4. How many disciples did Jesus have?

5. How many fishes did Jesus use to feed 5,000 people?

6. How many days was Lazarus dead when Jesus raised him up?

7. How many loaves did Jesus use to feed 5,000 people?

8. How many disciples were left after Judas died?

9. How many days was Jesus in the grave?

10. Jesus healed ten lepers. How many did not thank him?

11. On which day did God rest after creating everything?

12. When Jesus arose, how many days before Thomas saw him?

___
F

___
A

___
J

___
L

___
B

___
D

___
E

___
K

___
C

___
I

___
G

___
H

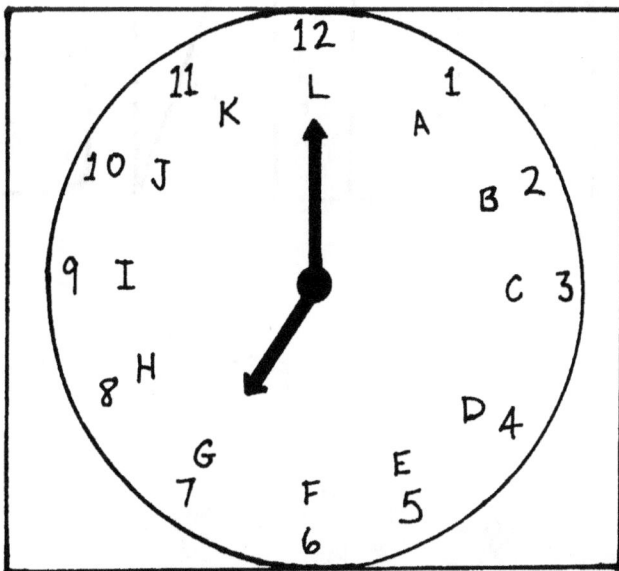

6. Who Loves To Do Good Things For You?

Someone strong and mighty loves to do good things for you. Who is he? Draw lines between the matching shapes. Copy the letters in the correct shapes. Whose name have you spelled?

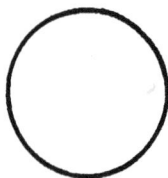

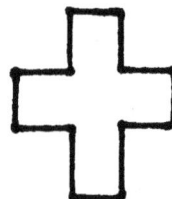

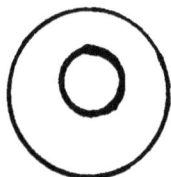

What Is Too Hard For God To Do?

Trace the letters in the word below to find the answer.

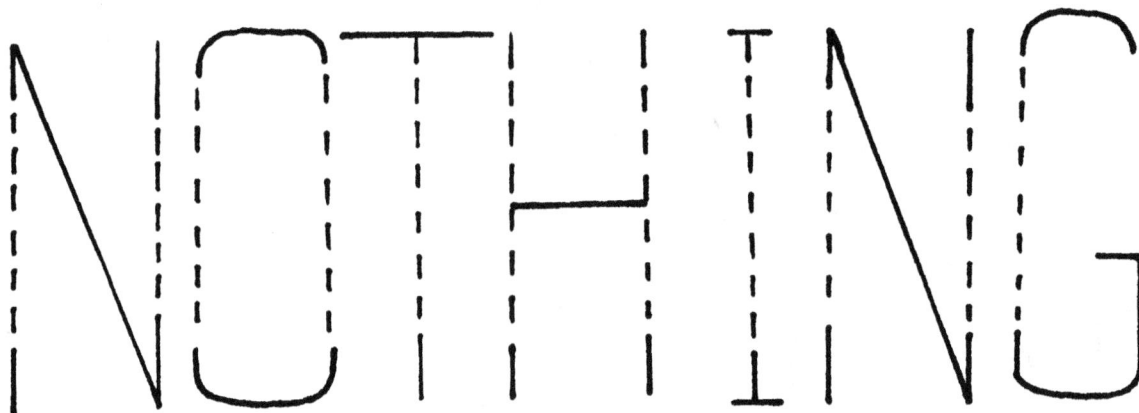

NOTHING

(Read Jeremiah 32:17 to the class.)

7. The Empty Tomb

"Jesus' tomb is empty!" Mary Magdalene said to Peter and John. They ran to see it. Help them find the way there. Use a pencil first. Don't pass over a bar across the way. When you have found the right way, mark the path with a red crayon.

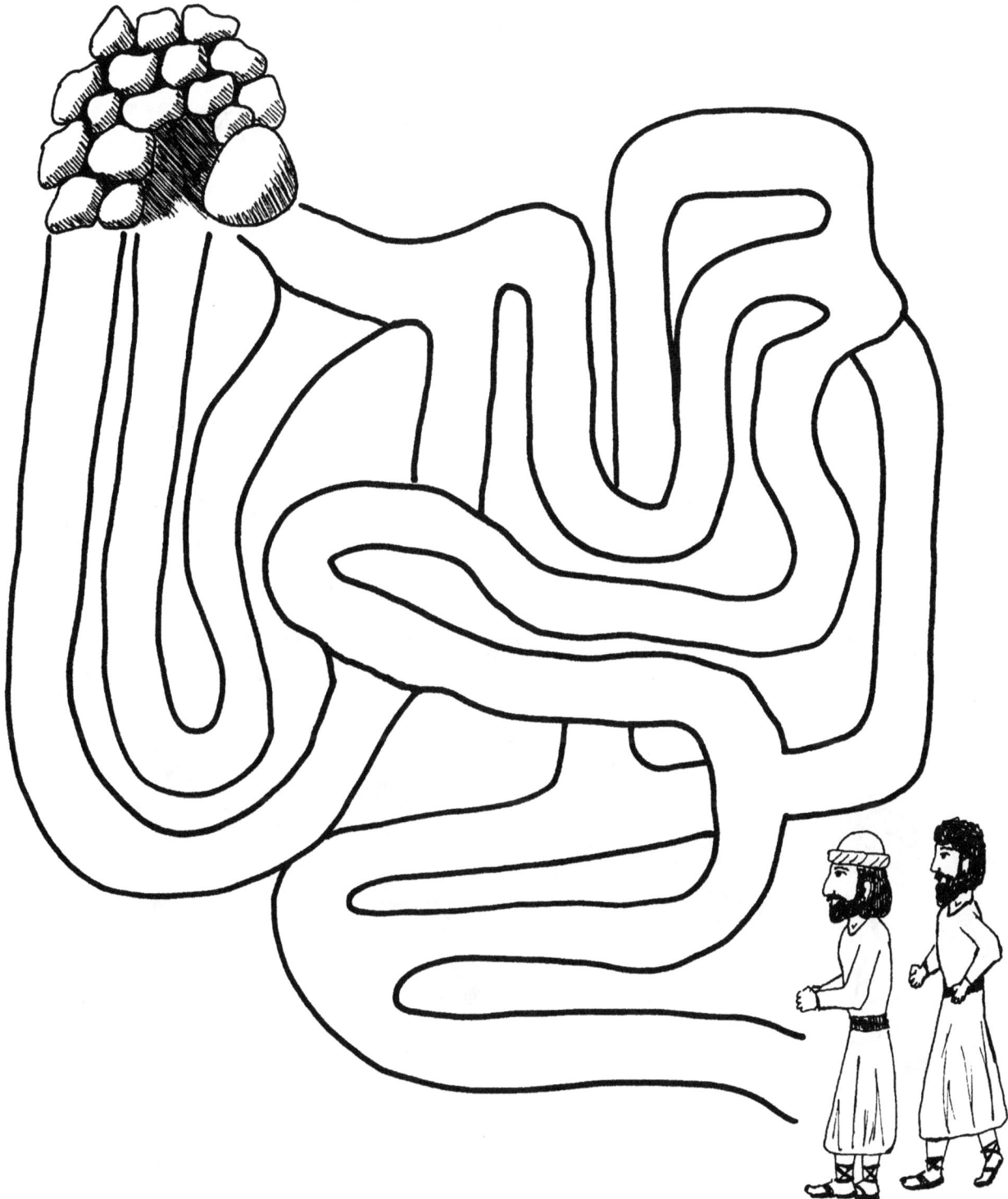

8. The Sheep And The Children

Color the sheep. Circle the ones who are going the right way.

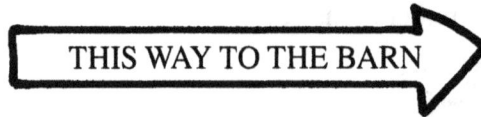

Who watches the sheep and knows where they are going? (The word is spelled backwards. Write the letters in the right order.) The DREHPEHS __ __ __ __ __ __ __ __ sees the sheep.

Color the children. Circle those who are going the right way.

Who sees the children and knows what they are doing? __ __ __.

1. Mountain Climber
(Haggai 1 and 2)

Materials Needed
Duplicated copies of the Mountain Climber game, file folders, small envelopes, pennies, construction paper, index cards, black crayon, glue.

Preparation
Duplicate one game and set of playing instructions for every two to six players. Cut these out and glue them to the inside of a file folder, as illustrated. Glue a small envelope inside the folder for holding the markers and cards.

For each game: Make playing cards by cutting eighteen index cards in half. With a black crayon, write either 1, 2, or 3 on each one (twelve of each number). For markers (one per player), draw around a penny on six different colors of construction paper, cut out the circles, and glue each to a penny.

Before playing the game the first time, and occasionally after that, tell the story, "Build God's House."

Build God's House
God's people, the Israelites, sinned against God. "Turn from your sin and obey me," God said, "or I will send a king to take you far away." But the Israelites kept on sinning. So the bad king came and took most of them to his land, far away.

After a long, long time, God let some of the Israelites come home to their own country again.

"Look! The bad king's soldiers burned down our houses!" they said. They came to where God's House used to be. "Look!" they cried. "The soldiers burned down God's House, too!"

"Build my House again," God said.

"It is not time to build God's House," the people told each other. They built fine houses for themselves. They went to work every day. They hurried back to their fine homes. But they did not build God's House. God waited and waited for a very long time. Still, they did not build it.

The people planted seed for crops. God did not send rain. The plants did not come up. They had no crops. They had no food. And they did not have enough money.

God sent Preacher Haggai to them. "Why don't you have enough food or money?" asked Haggai. "It is because you did not build God's House. Go up to the mountains. Cut down trees. Bring the wood and build God's House."

This time, the people obeyed God. They climbed the mountains. Puff, puff, puff! They cut down trees. Chop, chop, chop! They carried the heavy wood down the mountains. Puff, puff, puff! They worked hard and began to build God's House.

"Now I will bless you," said God. He sent the rain. The people planted seeds, and their crops grew. Everyone had food to eat. They had other things they needed, too. And then they knew that God's House is the most important house of all.

Play The Game

1. Tell the children they will pretend to be the Israelites, climbing a mountain and bringing down the wood to build the House of God.

2. Seat each two to six players on the floor or at a table. Place a game board in the center. If possible, have one adult to supervise each group of players. Give each player in the group a marker of a different color. Follow the instructions.

Mountain Climber Instructions

1. Place all markers at START. Put the cards in a pile nearby, face down. Decide who will begin. Take turns, going clockwise around the group. At each turn, a player draws one card from the pile and moves his marker the number of spaces it says. If he lands on a black space, he must go back one space. Continue playing until all players have finished.

2. Place all cards that are drawn in a discard pile. If all cards are drawn before the game is over, shuffle the cards in the discard pile and use them again.

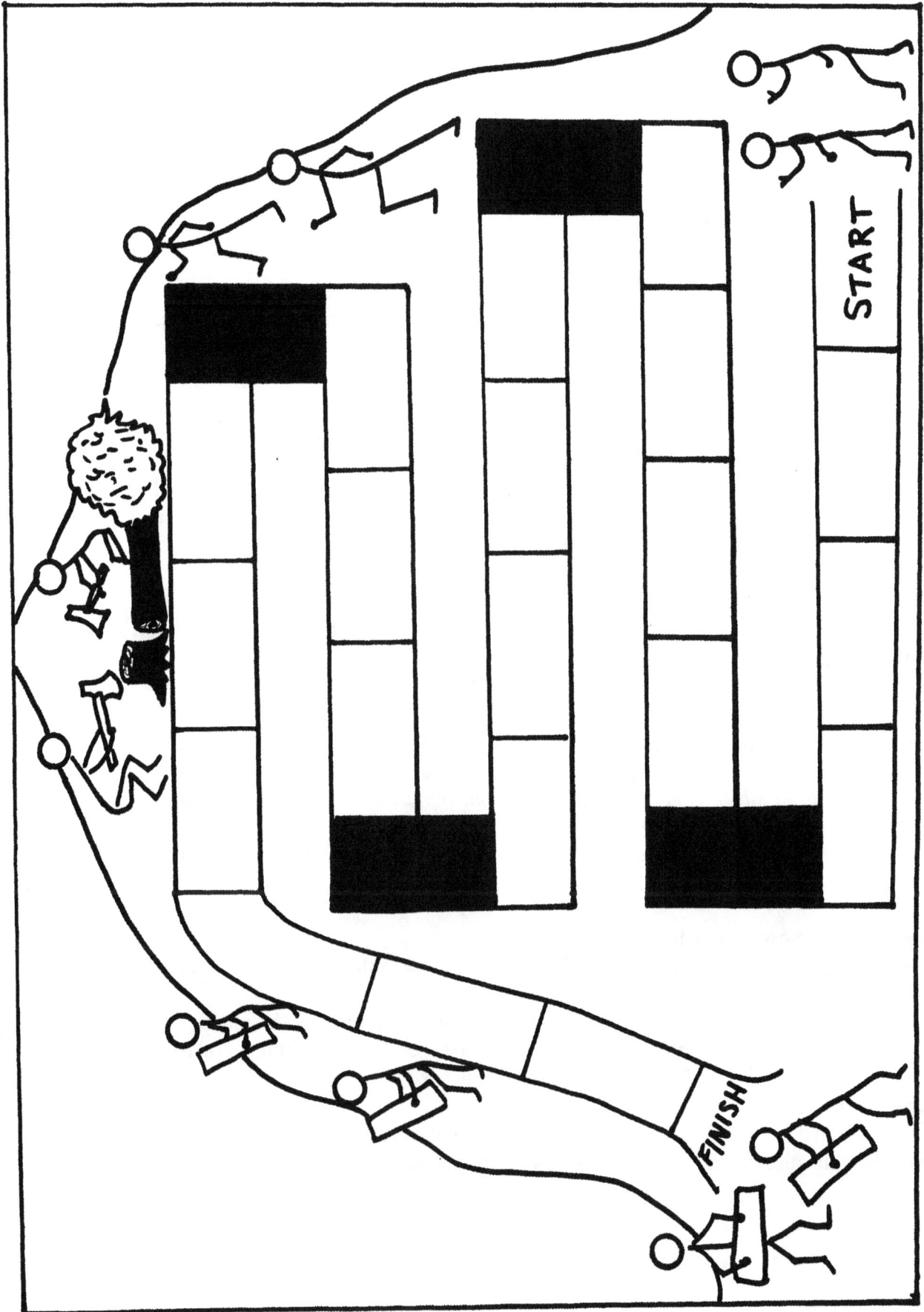

START

FINISH

2. Over The Rainbow

Purpose

To review three memory verses at once. This game may be used many times for any kind of memory work.

Materials Needed

Duplicated copies of the game sheet and playing instructions, file folders, small envelopes, construction paper, index cards, pennies, black crayon, other crayons or paints (optional), glue.

Preparation

Duplicate one game sheet and one set of instructions for every three to six players. Color the rainbows, if desired. Glue each sheet to the inside right of a file folder. On the left side, glue the playing instructions and an envelope (face down) for holding the game pieces.

For each game: Make playing cards by cutting eighteen index cards in half. With a black crayon, write either 1, 2, or 3 on each one (twelve of each number). For markers (one per player), draw around a penny on six different colors of construction paper, cut out the circles, and glue each to a penny.

Before Playing

Give each memory verse a number (1, 2, or 3). Holding up three index cards with those numbers, review the memory verses until the children associate the verse with the number.

Play The Game

Hold up the rainbow and point to the Bible at its end. Say, *Some people say there is a pot of gold at the end of a rainbow. Of course, that is not true. When you learn Bible verses, though, you gain something far better than gold or silver. God's Word stored in your mind can help you many times in life.* Read Psalm 119:127.

You should have an adult supervisor for each game. Seat 2 to 6 players at a table or on the floor. Place a game board in the center. Give each player in the group a marker of a different color. Follow the instructions.

Over The Rainbow Instructions

1. All players place their markers on or beside the arrow at the beginning of the rainbow. Put the cards in a pile nearby, face down. Decide who will begin.

2. The first player draws a card from the center pile and looks at the number. If he can repeat the memory verse for it, he may move his marker to the first space with that number on it. If not, he can't move until his turn comes again. (The youngest players may need to hear the first word of the verse or have help in recognizing the numbers.)

3. Place all cards that are drawn in a discard pile. If all cards are drawn before the game is over, shuffle the cards in the discard pile and use them again. Continue until all players reach the end of the rainbow.

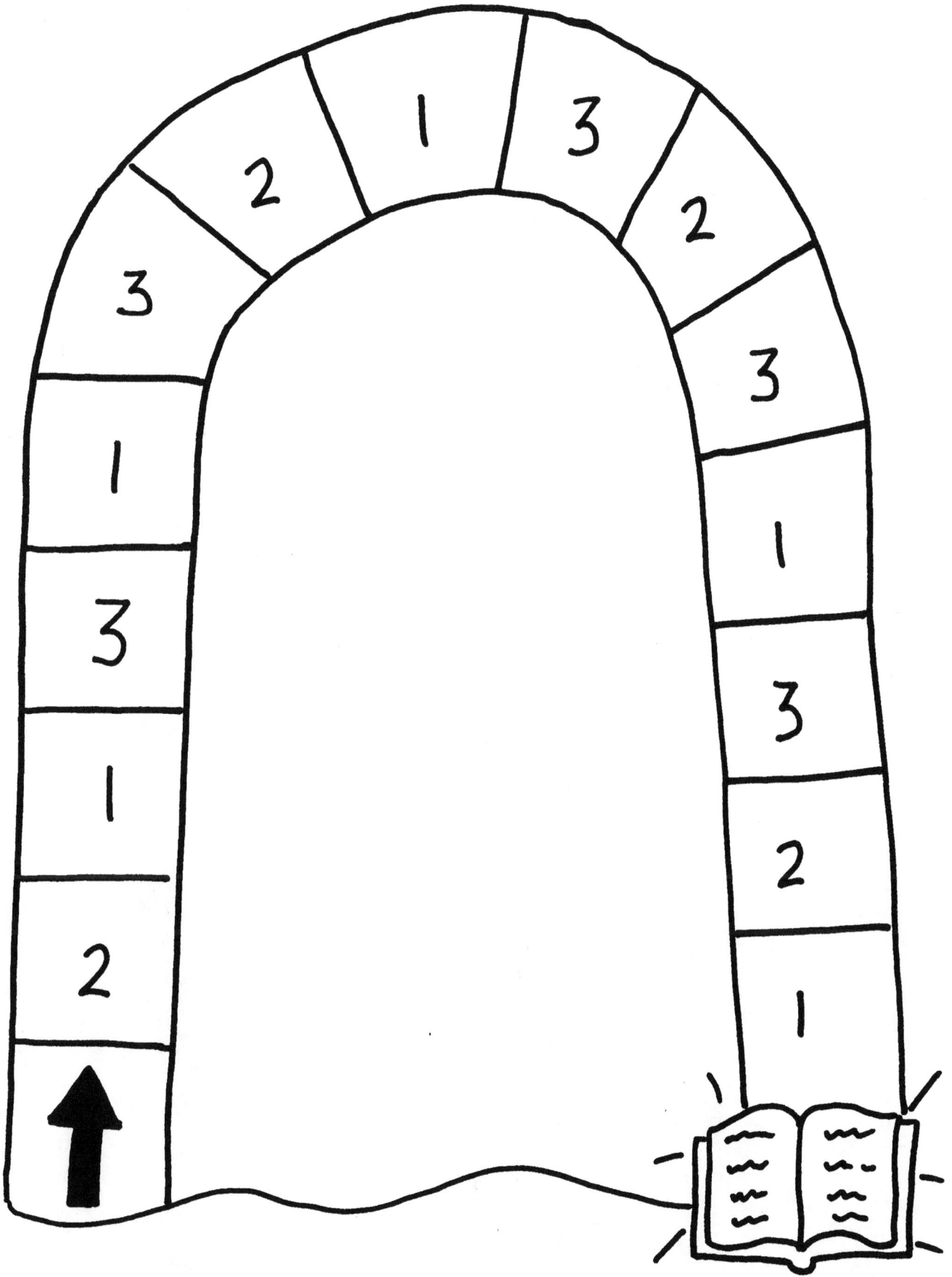

The Totally Terrific Award

is presented to

_____

for good work in

_____

_____

Signed

Answers

Page 49
1. 0 children
2. 1 child
3. 6 children

Page 51
1. glad
2. glad
3. glad
4. glad
5. mad
6. sad
7. glad
8. glad

Page 52
A cross
me

Page 54
God
Nothing

Page 56
Sheep:
Right way — 1, 2, 4
Wrong way — 3, 5
Shepherd

Children:
Right way — 2, 3, 4
Wrong way — 1, 5
God

www.ingramcontent.com/pod-product-compliance
Lightning Source LLC
Chambersburg PA
CBHW050356100426

42739CB00015BB/3422